LET'S TALK ABOUT CHURCH STAFF RELATIONSHIPS

LET'S TALK ABOUT CHURCH STAFF RELATIONSHIPS

by

Ronald W. Wiebe
Bruce A. Rowlison

Copyright © 1983 by Ronald W. Wiebe and
Bruce A. Rowlison

All rights reserved. No part of this book may be used or reproduced in any manner whatsoever without written permission, except in the case of brief quotations embodied in critical articles and reviews.

ISBN 0-938462-12-1

Green Leaf Press, P.O. Box 6880, Alhambra, CA 91801

PRINTED IN THE UNITED STATES OF AMERICA

Table of Contents

	Contents	5
	Preface	7
I.	Expectations for the Senior Pastor	8
II.	Expectations for a Youth Pastor	12
III.	Double Binds of an Assistant/Associate	15
IV.	Power--Appropriate and Inappropriate Uses	19
V.	Conflict--Other Areas of Potential Tension	25
VI.	Difficult Multiple Staff Personalities	30
VII.	Selecting and Growing a Church Staff	40
VIII.	Important Things a Senior Pastor Can Do for an Associate/Assistant	46
IX.	Important Things an Assistant Can Do for a Senior Pastor	50
X.	Resolving Pastor, Painful Staff Relationships	53
XI.	Where is Hope?	55
	Epilogue	58
	Bibliography	59
	About the Authors	61

Acknowledgements

The preparation of this book has been a joint effort by the authors. We have enjoyed developing and maintaining an unusual quad-triple relationship: client-to-therapist, pastor-to-layman, friend-to-friend, professional co-authors.

We wish to thank Dr. Foster Shannon for considerable editorial work on the manuscript, as well as Mrs. Jo Apel for typing several revisions of the manuscript and for her able work on preparing the final copy for the printer. Graphics work has been competently done by Mrs. Anita Heihn. To our thirty pastor friends who freely shared their experiences and insights we owe a big debt.

Cartoons on pages 10, 16, 26, and 28 by Larry Thomas. Cartoons on pages 18, 42, and 48 by Bob Portlock. They have made a significant contribution in their cartoons.

Cover photograph from the February/March 1974, "Wittenburg Door," used by permission from Youth Specialities, El Cajon, California.

Preface

The purpose of this book is to promote healthy relationships on church staffs. We are not trying to teach pastors how to pray together, study the Bible together, or spiritualize their problems. We know that most people reading this book will have a good understanding of the Bible and a commitment to prayer. And we are assured that the Holy Spirit gives wisdom far beyond this book. Yet we hope this discussion will drive the reader to the scriptures, leading him or her to specific and increased prayer, and enable conversation among colleagues about these issues, as well as with God.

What we are trying to do is simple. We want to identify probable areas of difficulty in multiple staff relationships. Awareness is the first step toward resolution. Multiple staff relationships are frequently loaded with problems. In some cases, good pastors are being chewed up by staff tensions, and not by ministry. Churches are being robbed of an effective model for Christian living. They are witnessing a rending of community, rather than the building up of parish life.

We see multiple uses for this book. It will help seminary theology classes deal with the realities of life in a local parish. It will provide important preparation for persons serving as interns in local churches. It can serve as a discussion aid for staff meetings, or a series of pastors' and elders' seminars. Whatever the form in which it is used, we urge dialogue, prayer, internal reflection, the keeping of a journal, and searching of the scriptures. May God bless you in an exciting and demanding journey.

Spend a few minutes jotting down what you need to talk about when it comes to staff relationships.

I
Expectations for the Senior Pastor

EXPECTATIONS: understanding definitions for success...the verbalized ones, and then the real ones which are most important.

For the senior pastor: What does the church congregation want?
- visitation expert
- preacher-teacher
- administrator
- leader in community affairs
- skills as an evangelist
- trained counselor
- builder of community life in the parish
- sensitivity and compassion
- skills in youth ministries
- jack of all trades

As leadership on the ruling board changes each year, the priorities must be communicated again and again. The sign in a friend's office reads, "The greatest problem in communication is the illusion that it has already been achieved." The expectations need to be reiterated frequently. A minister should review this expectation list at least once a year in board meetings. He should explain it to every new membership class so they know what they can expect of him. It should be reviewed in staff meetings periodically.

In addition to the more visible expectations of a congregation of the pastor, there are some more sophisticated role expectations. How a pastor faces these *subtle expectations* is crucial.

1. For many people the pastor is a father replacement and, to make matters more complicated, it is a distorted father image they seek. Throughout history, the priest or pastor has been viewed as a supportive father figure to a congregation and community. He visits in the hospital and blesses buildings. But

some project punitive, non-trustworthy characteristics on the pastor because of a poor earthly father model. They are sure that the pastor doesn't care for them, and will abandon them at the first opportunity. The mobility of priests and pastors tends to reinforce this distortion. This father replacement need has increased with the multiplication of divorce in recent years. Children with an absent father, or cruel father, may look to their pastor as the model of what a father should be.

2. Some parishioners have the *non-verbalized expectation* of the pastor to pacify God for them so that they don't have to work so hard in their relationship with God. The logic is that the pastor lives his life near to God and is able to keep God at a distance so that God won't intrude himself in the layperson's life. Therefore, the pastor can't burp, or notice an attractive woman, or show other signs of humanness. After all, the pastor flies with angels.

3. What are the associate/assistant's expectations of you?
- to be available to them at any time
- to help them solve problems
- to disciple them...impart your wisdom and experience in a non-pompous way
- to give them lots of freedom to make mistakes
- to share your life with them (some level of intimacy beyond the congregation's relationship)
- to be open to their ideas and suggestions
- to father him or her

4. What are your non-negotiables as a pastor--places where you will exclaim, "Here I stand. I can do no other."? Perhaps it is your day off, style of worship service, doing no administration, no visitation. Where are you theologically flexible, and where are you rigid--baptism views, whom you marry and don't marry, how people become Christians?

5. How do you perceive your role in relationship to the leadership of the parish. Are you one of them, an equal with different responsibilities--their leader--or their employee? How you perceive yourself is crit-

"What makes you think I've got problems with my staff?"

cal to how you function. How would your confusion in this area impact your staff?

When I reflect on the variety of expectations placed on the senior pastor, the chief areas of confusion and conflict seem to be:

What rightful concerns of the congregation have you not recognized?

What non-negotiables have been inadequately communicated?

What contradictions (and possible conflicts) exist between the role expectations of the congregation on the one hand and members of the staff on the other?

II
Expectations for a Youth Pastor

It is important for a pastor working with young people to know the definitions of success in his church. Here are some interesting possibilities:

1. For the Christian Education Committee:
Many good things are happening, but how many young people are at each meeting?

2. For the Business Administrator or Treasurer:
Many good things may be happening, but how many young people are pledging to the church and how much?

3. For the Senior Pastor:
Many good things may be happening in youth ministry, but how many young people are in the worship services?

4. For the Church Secretary:
Many good things may be happening in youth ministry, but are you reaching my child?

5. For the Mission Committee:
You are having lots of Bible studies and socials, but how many young people are going out to the mission field?

6. For another:
Yes, but are the young people being changed into [my concept of] the image of Christ?

7. Add to the above expectation possibilities the expectation God has for us.

8. Then there is a spouse's expectation if one is married.
Every spouse comes into a marriage with certain role expectations from childhood. "My father was home on Friday nights, and took mom out to dinner on Sat-

urday nights. That's security and intimacy! Now I'm married to a guy who has wedding rehearsals on Friday nights, and prepares sermons every Saturday night. Why does my spouse nurture everybody else and not me? I married him because he was a caring person, and all he does is nurture others."

9. Our own children have another expectation of us.

"Why doesn't Daddy play ball with us in the evening like other fathers? He's always at meetings. Why can't he take me to football games on Sunday afternoons? Other daddies do."

10. We have our own expectation of ourself.

"Since I'm a pastor, I should become all that God wants of me," which is frequently translated into, "I have no personal needs. I should never tire of doing God's work."

The authors believe that when doing God's work exceeds a person's capacity and energy--it isn't God who is talking--but one's own expectations rooted in the past. God is not a cruel foreman.

If expectations are a major obstacle to healthy, satisfying staff relationships, here are four handles in building long-term relationships. They have been called the four predictable stages in such relationships:

1. Courtship
   You share information. You voice your expectations and negotiate.

2. Commitment
   You agree upon liveable expectations. You formalize your expectations.

3. Honeymoon
   You live in basic equilibrium. You get out of the relationship pretty much what you expected. You give to the relationship what you expected. This is a very stable and productive period.

4. Disruption of expectations
   You expect more of the other or something different or vice versa. Now you have three alternatives:
   a. Divorce--get out of the relationship (change churches or fire the other person)
   b. Kiss and make up (gloss over the expectation crisis and pretend it doesn't exist)
   c. Go back to step 1 and renegotiate your mutual expectations. We believe this alternative is best.

We realize some staff members will strongly resist renegotiating or modifying expectations. It is helpful to understand that you are always working your way through stages 1, 2, 3, or 4, and to recognize where you are in that process.

Recommended reading: *Why Christians Burn Out* by Charles E. Perry, Jr., Thomas Nelson, 1982, *Burn Out* by Dr. Herbert J. Freudenberger, Anchor Press/Doubleday, 1980.

III
Double Binds of an Assistant/Associate

A double bind is being caught between two immovable demands. It appears the conflicting demands cannot be resolved. The tragedy of double binding is that it immobilizes a person and creates a situation where people look for a scapegoat. An assistant pastor becomes the perfect candidate. "If only I had a competent staff, this church would be great," is the cry of many a senior pastor.

1. He or she has just gained independence from *old dad* through great struggle. They have barely had time to enjoy the feeling of freedom and individuality and independence. Now they are forced back into the parent-child relationship with:

   a. Senior pastor
   b. Church board
   c. His or her long-range professional hopes hanging in the balance
   d. God will get them if they are not being submissive to authority

2. The young pastor has been forced in seminary to think through his or her own theology...rewarded for doing so, and penalized for not framing his or her own theology. In many denominations framing one's own theology is a prerequisite for ordination. Now in direct violation of seminary training, one must accept another's theological structure.

3. One is also testing his adult and professional competence for the first time while these restraints pressure him from many sides. Plus, most of one's contemporaries have already established themselves, having been out of high school or college a number of years. Can I really make it in the pastorate, or do I need to change occupations?

"And in this week's drawing we have 7 weddings and 4 funerals!"

4. There is frequently role confusion which comes from a fluid job description. Therefore, substantial time and effort need to be spent on charting the assistant pastor's needs alongside the church's needs. The job description is often contradictory. An illustration of this is on Thursday afternoon when the senior pastor expects him to teach the senior citizen's class, the board wants him to do hospital visitation, his children want him to coach their football team, his wife wants him to do none of the above, and his need is to write in his journal. One can feel the conflict in the different expectations which will have considerable impact on one's self perception. These inconsistencies are a major factor leading to the present, popular expression of *burn out*.

5. The youth or assistant pastor has the two immovable demands of choosing either a multiple staff relationship with all its complicated struggles or the loneliness and solitude of a little isolated parish that will accept someone just out of seminary. The problem of learning by experience is that you get the test first and then the lesson. That can prove to be an even tougher and more painful teacher than the struggles of a multiple staff relationship.

6. Often the assistant pastor, recently out of seminary, continues to grow spiritually and begins to understand that his spiritual gifts and priorities do not fit the hopes or job description expectations of the senior pastor. At the same time, he is gradually developing great confidence and significant ministry in other areas of church life.

"I've **done** it!! I've created the perfect assistant pastor!"

IV
Power--Appropriate and Inappropriate Uses

The *Christian Leadership* letter of October 1982, states that the idea of power is inherent in all organizations. Yet, it is one of the least understood ideas of organizational life. In order for society or an organization like a church to function, there has to be authority. Yet, we vacillate one moment denying the reality of power in the church, and the next moment being afraid of it--and then being caught up in the struggle to accumulate more power. Power is frequently conceived of as force, domination, or manipulation. In the church raw power is seldom used. However, domination is fairly common where those highest in authority request or command certain things done.

Manipulation is a common use of power in the church--where one gets others to do things without explicitly telling them.

Now take a close look at your church. How has power been exercised? If it has a history of manipulation and your style is domination, go slowly. A number of Christian leaders have compared power in the church to an iceberg--7/8 of the struggle and danger lies below the observable surface. (*Leadership Magazine*, Vol. 1, #1, Spring 1980.) That is why we raise the following questions.

There is a subtlety of power to look for in a church. The one who appears to have the power often really has little, and the one who appears to be powerless often has the power. We had an elder who was relatively new to the church, but his sincerity and eagerness got him elected to the board. He mumbled as he spoke so you had to sit on the edge of your seat to understand what he said. When the board voted against his wishes, he went around talking to people about how hard he worked in the church (which was true) and how they hurt his feelings. For two and one half years he was "the" leader of the church. He determined policy and direction because the staff and board were afraid of "hurting his feelings" or "making him angry." Few people looking at the church would say this *inarticulate and insecure* man was single handedly setting the direction of the entire church.

The alcoholic who appears weak, mousy, insecure, and timid has the whole family revolving around him. The "emotionally ill" seem to have our whole legal system revolving around them. They are often let off without responsibility for their crimes because of "sickness." The little kid who kicks the waste baskets has the whole family jumping to carry out his commands. Who is getting his wishes in the church every time a vote is taken? It may not be the strong, confident, wise, or godly.

Power is not the attribute of a person, but the property of a relationship. If the highway patrolman pulls over a professor for driving too fast, the patrolman has the power. The next night, in extension school, the professor smiles as the highway patrolman walks into class and takes his seat. Change the relationship and the power shifts.

An outstanding pastor, with great insight, recognized this when he said to the board as he left a large, prestigious church, "You don't have to get a well known, popular preacher. Get a man of God who will meet your needs. This church and this pulpit will make the man famous."

Where does the power lie in this church?

How are decisions made?

Who makes them?

Who carries them out?

Is the board advisory, supportive, influential, or directing?

Here are some illustrations:

1. In one church, the power resided in the church secretary whose father founded the church.

2. In another church, the power was in the administrator who had the task of carrying out most executive decisions.

Much power is in *the pulpit* and worship experience. If a counselor, evangelist, missionary, intern, or seminarian comes on staff, it greatly aids that ministry if he/she can speak weekly in worship if only for three minutes. That gives exposure, validity, strength, full acceptance to that person. We prefer to have them preach the first or second Sunday. If such a person can't preach well, then we use interviews, visual aids, and other opportunities. We humorously refer to this in staff meetings as "face time," "up front time," "visibility," or "exposure." The dilemma is that most senior pastors get about eighty percent of their affirmation from up front preaching. Their identity is often wrapped up in it. Therefore, they are reluctant to share the pulpit.

Case Study: The associate pastor was given absolutely no time to preach. There was little or no communication with the senior pastor on critical issues. Both were extremely afraid of confronting each other, hoping that neither would agitate the other. We encouraged them to openly communicate, resulting in the associate pastor's sharing his personal need. This sharing was received warmly by the senior pastor and four preaching times per year were arranged, much to the satisfaction of the associate.

The church newsletter is an important source of power. An assistant minister was not permitted to preach except once a year on Youth Sunday, so he asked for a two-paragraph column--ten sentences--in the weekly church newsletter. That gave additional strength to his ministry, and people stopped asking him what he did with all his time.

3. In still another church, the power was with the nationally known choir director.

4. Another church had a wealthy layman who gave large sums of money, which made him the decision maker in the church boards.

Power Lines

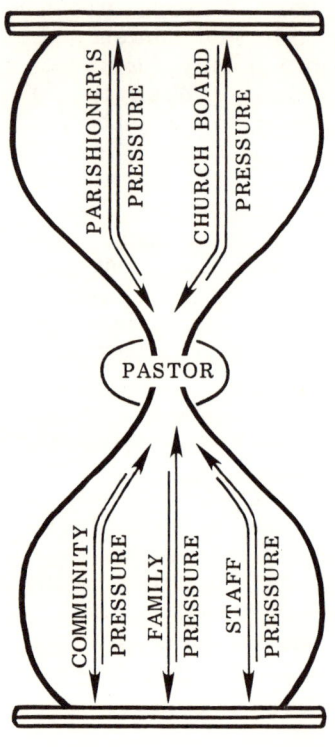

The pastor stands in the middle of the hour glass, with sand flowing in all directions. He determines which way the sand will flow, and when.

The sand is communication flow, problem-solving flow, administrative decision-making flow, emotional and spiritual nurture flow, financial flow.

If an assistant pastor doesn't understand this dynamic, he is in trouble. He needs to know who nurtures whom, and how. He needs to know how the board puts subtle pressures on the senior pastor and sways him/her. He needs to know the effect of community pressure on the church. How do parishioners communicate with the pastor--through the secretary, the pastor's wife, a memo?

The pastor's office is definitely a place of power. Is that where staff meetings are held? How large is the desk? Who leads the staff meetings? Are decisions made there or over coffee?

Case study on power: The associate pastor functioned well, at least on the surface, for one and a half years, never telling anyone that he and his wife could not tolerate the theological presuppositions of the senior pastor. When a second associate was placed on the staff, the first associate soon discovered that the second associate supported his theological views. This then started a power play as the two of them decided to approach the board of elders, hoping that they would have enough support to force a position change of the senior pastor. Unfortunately, they did not do their homework, and they soon discovered that the board of elders supported the senior pastor completely. There was no desire for problem solving on the part of the board, senior pastor, nor the associates, and the associates were soon on their way to other churches.

Case study on power: The associate pastor left after only a few months. He came from a seminary where team relationships, or more formally a mangement-by-objective approach was used as an administrative model. This associate came to a church where the senior pastor had been running what would be called a benevolent dictatorship for ten years and he was not about to change. He made all decisions and his board functioned more as an advisory committee to the senior pastor. The associate could not tolerate this form of government, and he left without either pastor desiring a problem-solving approach.

Final Reflections on Power

Philippians 2 and John 13 and the cross of Christ give us a portrait of power. Instead of "lording" it over us, God chooses to come under us as a servant. The incarnation upsets our commonly held world view that the greatest power is brute force over a weaker subject.

Ephesians 1:19,20 links the power of the disciples to the power of Christ. The church and Christ's disciples are given his resurrected power to carry out their tasks.

Power does not reside inherently in one's self or as an effect of one's effort. It is a trust given from God. Therefore, we need to learn how to live as custodians of power. The more we mistake the basis of our power the more likely we are to be corrupt in the way we exercise it.

Power is entrusted to you *to build up the body of Christ*, just as spiritual gifts are given to individuals for the good of the church.

How much power do you now have?

How much power do you want?

What will be the consequences of achieving that power?

V
Conflict——Other Areas of Potential Tension

Conflict is any ongoing struggle, clash, contention, antagonism, incompatibility, opposition between different interests, personalities, ideas. When these issues are resolved or endured in love they can be valuable in building the church--exciting and vital signs that the church is alive. On the other hand, if the conflict is protracted and destructive the problem is serious. Some contend that the instant solutions given to every problem in life in 30 to 60 minute television programs have reduced our ability to cope with conflict. Computers and jet planes have speeded up many processes--but problem-solving in human relationships takes at least as much time as it did in the day of the apostle Paul.

1. There may be conflict if the assistant pastor is or appears to be more spiritual than the pastor.

2. The possibility of conflict arises if there develops great differences in energy level...such as, a young assistant who is out conquering the world and a pastor near retirement, with less energy.

Case study: In this particular church the senior pastor, approximately in his late fifties, decided that the church membership was growing old with him and he decided to hire a young, dynamic associate pastor to bring young people into the church. The associate pastor was so good at his work that the church membership soon found itself with over fifty percent of college age students. The two groups, the college age and those over fifty (very few were in their thirties or forties) began to find need differences, theological differences, and so forth, and--although the pastors seemed to get along--increasing tension occurred within the church body. The board of elders decided that the pressure was too great to resolve and a new church started only a few blocks away with the younger membership making the change of location.

"They're 'casting lots' to see who goes with the junior high kids to camp."

3. Conflict often arises if there is a preconceived notion that "this is my field," and suddenly there is an overlap of roles. "Why are you doing my work when you should be attending to your responsibilities?"

4. Conflict arises if each staff member has the same gifts. We set them up for competition...more people go to him for counseling than to me, or more attend his Bible studies than mine.

5. Expect an explosion if you insist on staffing the church with two powerful, dynamic, headstrong pastors with enormous charisma--and both are used to large followings. Remember that somebody has to be in the wings to open and close the curtain and change the props. Two "center stage" is more than most relationships and churches can survive.

6. What happens when you are assigned a gift of administration by the senior pastor when you never knew you had that gift--God has never told you that is your gift?

7. What happens if one of the pastors gets the gift of tongues and "feels" or "has a leading" to take the church toward the charismatic stance? One pastor claims he is led by the word of God, and the other claims he is led by the Holy Spirit!

8. What happens if the assistant arrives only to discover that the senior pastor is God's unique gift to the church and the entire membership is the senior pastor's fan group?

9. If an assistant challenges the system, he moves from a green light area to a yellow light area--meaning, he doesn't know if he's coming or going.
   Why do you have an evening service for 33 people?
   Why are we so formal on Sunday morning?
   Why do you preach with a full manuscript?
   Why are decisions really made before staff ever meets, or outside of the board meetings?
   Why are sermons so abstract and impersonal?

"I want you all to remember that we are a team."

10. A church sets itself up for conflict when it doesn't have a good communication system. There need to be staff meetings, memos, parties, and other opportunities for interaction. Especially important are staff meetings before and after board meetings. During the period of time this book was written, one of the authors found that forty percent of churches he consulted had no weekly system for bringing staff together to share, problem-solve, plan ahead, and pray for each other.

11. Conflict can occur when a person does not work through their needing to be a pastor: needing an audience, needing to be up front, needing to perform, and needing to be needed.

12. Destructive conflict is built into the style of a senior pastor who keeps saying to his assistants:
"Wow, we sure need a young couples' club in this church!"
"Wow, we certainly need more aggressive visitation of church visitors!"
"Wow, this isn't getting done in the parish."
All of this means, "Get on it, Charlie!"

In summary, when a senior pastor keeps pushing his guilt on his associates, be prepared for an explosion.

13. Stereotyping is another factor which sets church staffs up for unnecessary conflict.
"All Irish priests have tempers."
"All Baptist ministers are legalistic."
"All associate pastors are so green that they have to be closely supervised on everything they do."

Along with stereotyping, the practice of scapegoating destroys church staffs: The senior pastor makes it look like all problems in the church are the assistant pastor's fault...and takes credit for the good things.

14. Staff disruptions occur on any issue for change if a member of the staff does not get sanction for change from all persons impacted.

VI
Difficult Multiple Staff Personalities

Pastors often find themselves baffled by the behavior of their colleagues. They try a number of approaches to communicate and develop a better working relationship. "What kind of behavior is this? Where did it come from? What is my responsibility in working alongside it? Do I ignore it? Do I strike out at it? Do I continue hoping it changes? My field is theology, not psychology. I'm confused. Their behavior is reducing my effectiveness."

Here is our thesis: *TO RELATE SUCCESSFULLY AS A PART OF A MULTIPLE STAFF TEAM REQUIRES SPECIAL SKILLS that all ordained persons don't possess, and some never will because they don't want to.* This does not mean certain people are "bad" or "unfit for ministry," but we seriously question whether a multiple staff position is for them. Some ought to be set free to do theological research, others as itinerant teachers, evangelists, or preachers who do not have to relate to peers in the stress of multiple staff situations. Another solution is for such individuals to remain in a small church.

Case study: Father Robert is in an Episcopal parish near San Diego. At forty years of age and the senior pastor of a large staff, he has distinguished himself in preaching and teaching. One hundred people come repeatedly to his morning study. He repeats the phenomenon weekly at a parish in a nearby city. When people invite him to dinner, come to his study for counseling, or expect any kind of personal relationship, they go away let down. He is unable to listen, express empathy, give or receive affection, affirm people, or be comfortably present at any pastoral event. Only a "chosen few," which he carefully selects, get as close as he determines.

To say his associates and assistants are frustrated is an understatement. Yet, unless his reputation as a Bible teacher continues to increase and he becomes a better known superstar, the bishop will leave him in a parish to confuse and baffle staff associates and parishioners.

Most of us operate under the assumption that with a little more love, a little more understanding, a little more prayer, a little more time for God to do a miracle, a little more..., any personalities can work together. We, the authors, believe that too. If we will focus on our primary task and set aside our personal needs, we can work together in a multiple staff parish relationship. But, if people persist in maintaining certain personality characteristics, which are destructive to a team ministry, then it will be very difficult to work with them. It might become necessary to remove such persons from the staff in order to preserve the wellbeing of the church. There comes a time when the church must be defended.

All personal characteristics are not to be discarded, only modified or set aside for the sake of the church.

Let's look at eight difficult multiple staff relationships.

1. Humble Harry/Dependable David/Adaptable Ann
This type of individual exhibits the very model of humility, servanthood, and desire to give of one's own life. They adapt easily to please people to such an extent that they do not want to face the fact that they may displease others.

They avoid asserting themselves since they do not want to appear to be aggressive, which they believe to be sinful. They seem extremely sensitive and cannot tolerate criticism. Their humility is actually a denial of their accomplishments. This is due to lack of self esteem. Whatever self esteem they have is largely developed from the feedback of others. They are not able to draw support from their own emotional reservoir and, therefore, need a constant supply of nurturing from the people in their environment.

By turning their energies toward other people for emotional sustenance, they leave themselves at the mercy of the feelings and emotions of others. This leaves them essentially defenseless as they have eliminated their own free will or given it to others upon whom they are dependent for social approval.

The senior pastor may find such a person quick to submit to his requests. Although this may be pleasing at first, such ready compliance becomes a problem because the individual is fearful to think for himself. This kind of person tends to look for an all-powerful father-figure in which he can place his trust. This dependency carries the hope that the senior pastor will give protection from external pressures. They are afraid to assume responsibility which may subject them to rejection through evaluation.

The answer is to assist such persons to give up their dependency habits. Building a self image of competence is required. This is a slow, step-by-step process in which the individual must perceive a strengthening of his attributes and overcome the practice of leaning on others.

It is suggested that the senior pastor allow this type of associate to lean on his strength and authority during the slow process of growth. This will enable him to be a sociable person and give affection and affirmation to others. The danger is that he will withdraw into himself once such support is removed.

2. Magic Mac
In another situation, the senior pastor may find an associate who generally resists any kind of confrontation and insight, and who will change only following periods of extreme social pressures. Such persons attempt to perceive life in magical solutions and, in general, have poor judgment--substituting the playing of hunches for sound reasoning. Such individuals dramatize their problems and are generally over-emotional. They are hyper-alert, so much so, that they overgeneralize the moods and behavior of others. Their behavior is overly reactive, dramatic, and extremely expressive. They crave stimulation and excitement, and quickly become bored with normal routines.

Their ability to develop quick friendships may

appear to be a positive characteristic. However, they are often either demanding and inconsiderate, or they may be extremely manipulative of these friendships.

There is very little hope for change in this personality structure unless the individual becomes aware of his destructiveness and is willing to learn objectivity through working with an associate. Even after some progress has been made, there may be regression to former unhealthy patterns.

3. Super-Strong, Self-Centered Steve

Another problem personality is that of persons who have almost the opposite characteristics of those described in the previous pages. Such individuals have a great fear of loss of self-determination. They try to enhance themselves by proudly displaying their achievements and try to be stronger and more important than other people. They seem to overvalue their personal worth, and direct their affection toward themselves rather than others. They expect others to cater to their false pride or self-esteem. Unfortunately, this form of self-assurance is admired in our present society, although it is not in harmony with the Bible. This individual's illusion of specialness is so exaggerated that it grates on others. There is a sense of grandiose self-importance. When goals are pursued there is an internal ambition that cannot be satisfied.

One of the biggest supervisory problems is negative response to criticism or any kind of disappointment. Their tendency to disregard the rights of others can be destructive to the church. Further problems with supervising this type of individual are involved in their resistance to personal exploration. They become indignant over confrontation regarding deficiencies. Their exaggerated sense of self-importance leads them to believe they do not need guidance by "less talented" persons.

4. Conforming, Compulsive Carl

We now come to a personality characteristic that may be desired by the senior pastor so that he seeks out such persons for his staff. These individuals are overly conforming and adhere to societal rules and customs to such an extent that they not only abide by them, but may embellish them. Such persons are often seen as moralistic, self-righteous, and legalistic. They are meticulous in their work patterns, and can get totally absorbed in detail far beyond what is required. They are extremely devoted to work and productivity to the point of eliminating pleasure. This can lead to the problem of burn out.

Although this appears to be the kind of person we would like to hire, often underneath this behavior is insecurity, anger, and bitterness. They do not dare take the chance of exposing themselves to others, since their resentment may be exposed. Unfortunately, their need for perfection interferes with their ability to grasp a healthy way of living, and they insist that others respond to their way of doing things.

Supervisory problems become evident as these individuals avoid exploring and risk taking. They are not only reluctant, but often obstinate about making changes in their lives. As long as they are well prepared for the tasks they face, it is likely that they will remain personable and well functioning in their daily work tasks.

The senior pastor must keep in mind that stability for them equals a well-ordered life. If unanticipated problems or job demands occur, such persons may begin to deteriorate. They defend themselves skillfully and, only after building a close trust relationship will they begin to talk about their resentments and insecurity. For every pound of risk they take in exposing themselves, their mentors must bolster their perception of self-adequacy by an equal pound.

INTERLUDE

The four personality patterns just described may be extremely difficult, if not impossible, to work with. The next four personality types are somewhat less difficult, and hold somewhat more favorable possibilities for improvement. Such persons can begin to change if they recognize the reality of their personality problems, and are willing to respond to supervision.

Sometimes such personality difficulties must be referred to Christian counselors and psychotherapists for more extensive work in order to make positive changes. *A Consumer's Guide to Christian Counseling* by Dr. John E. Roe, Abingdon Press, 1982, is a valuable resource. If these individuals are not willing to respond in a positive manner it may be necessary to remove them from the church staff. Or you, as an assistant, may need to get out of the present staff situation and request a change of parish.

We all may have some of these characteristics. There are no pure personality patterns. They overlap. And at times we all are a little self-centered, wishing for magical solutions, compulsive, moody, and negative. It is when these tendencies are endemic and pronounced that serious problems develop.

We are not usurping the work of the Holy Spirit, nor are we downgrading the change a Christ-centered life will bring. Healing can and does occur in the church environment. The tragedy is that it is the experience of psychotherapists that some of these people are highly resistant to change.

The issue is: Are they willing to self-reflect on and change their behavior?

5. Moody Mike or Negative Ned
Let us go on to another personality type that is likely to be disruptive to work relationships. We tend to regard such individuals as "emotionally immature." They are frequently irritable and erratically moody, and have a tendency to be easily frustrated and angry. They feel unappreciated, pessimistic, disgruntled, and disillusioned with life, and habitually resent demands to maintain a certain consistent level of functioning.

These individuals indirectly resist supervision through such maneuvers as procrastination, stubbornness, intentional inefficiency, and forgetfulness. Their childlike and unpredictable behaviors constantly intrude into their everyday life, resulting in a general unpredictability. They cannot decide whether to adhere to the desires of others as a means of gaining comfort and security, or to turn to themselves for such nurture. They vascillate between taking control of their lives or sitting by idly, letting others do their work for them. Unfortunately, such individuals may deteriorate emotionally into extreme anxiety and/or depressive disorders.

As in other personality problems, such persons must begin to recognize the destructive nature of their ambivalence and be willing to develop a more consistent approach to life.

6. Private Patrick

This type of person views supervision as signifying weakness and dependency. Such individuals are usually arrogant and intimidating, and the supervisor will frequently be subjected to demeaning comments. If you are friendly and sympathetic to these individuals, they view this as deceitful. However, if you are direct, cool, indifferent, and "straight" with them, this may drive them to creating new rationalizations about how people do not like them. *The supervisor must build trust over a long, slow period with an attitude of genuine respect for the individual.*

Somehow, these people must learn to share their anxieties with another person without feeling they will be harmed. The supervisor must accept who they are, but not conform to their beliefs.

As soon as this individual can begin to trust, the next level of desired behavior is their ability to accept ideas and suggestions from others.

These individuals are constantly concerned with hidden motives and special meanings. They are usually argumentative, make mountains out of molehills, and find it difficult to relax. They have no true sense of humor and appear cold to others. At the same time, they may view themselves as being objective. They lack tender feelings. There is no willingness to compromise, and there is an excessive need to be self-sufficient.

An extremely difficult part of supervision (or role modeling on the part of the pastor trying to demonstrate the fruit of the Spirit) is their disdain for people who are seen as soft, loving, and giving of themselves. They basically mistrust others, and desire to stay free of relationships since they might lose the power of self-determination. Minor criticism is viewed as an attack, and they are usually hypervigilant, which leads to blaming others when it is unwarranted. This drives other people away from them, which then substantiates their belief that other people do not care about them and are not to be trusted.

This personality pattern is becoming much more frequent in our society. It is associated with the general breakdown in family structure. Individuals who do not have healthy role models, from both a mother and father, are candidates for this personality development.

7. Loner Louis/Suspicious Stephanie

Occasionally we encounter individuals who are distinctively aloof, introverted, and seclusive. They appear to gain little satisfaction in personal relationships. Although this personality is usually not attracted to the ministry, it should be kept in mind. Occasionally someone is attracted to "lofty theology" as a kind of intellectual exercise. They often dislike the opposite sex. These people are unaware of the feelings and thoughts of others.

Although you may think that this person is rejecting or hostile, there is really a basic incapacity to sense the needs of others. They cannot form close, intimate relationships and not only is there an absence of tender feelings for others, but you will notice an indifference to the response of others to them. They prefer to be loners. They are withdrawn and usually pursue a solitary interest. They seem detached from their surroundings, and are vague about their goals in life. They seem self-absorbed in their own thoughts.

A slow introduction to socialization is necessary

and, although some intrusiveness is helpful, one has to be cautious or they will withdraw even further. A brief comment on this personality type is offered since the authors have observed this characteristic on a number of occasions in seminary students. It is assumed that these individuals eventually are encouraged to find other employment, or they disappear into the woodwork of some other profession, not being able to tolerate the social demands of the ministry.

8. Self-Focused Fred

The final destructive personality characteristic we choose to discuss is also on the increase. This person is incredibly self-centered and views everyone else as either an ally or enemy. An ally confirms their grandiosity--and an enemy threatens their self-perceived greatness.

Interaction with other people is only to get data and information to further their cause. Anyone not cooperating is devalued and persecuted.

This narcissistic person is usually very resistant to change. The rights of others are disregarded in order to indulge one's own desires. Others are taken advantage of for self-grandizement. Lack of the capacity for empathy is obvious. Self-esteem is built on a false or naive assumption of superiority. Any kind of dependency is viewed as a threat since this person has turned inward for self-esteem. The person is really saying, "My self-absorption is safe since I know how great I am, but I am not sure how you will treat me."

A severe blow in life will frequently find these individuals running for help. Their balloon has burst. The most help one can be at this time is to assist them to focus on their real attributes and competencies. By becoming more aware of reality, they are able to feel more in control, leading to a lesser need for false display of the self. Discovering how real God is, how real others are, and how someone can love even my realness, is a start in giving up this fragile veneer of strength. Unfortunately, few of these people will develop a desire for social cooperativeness. It is just too safe to love one's self.

SUMMARY

We have sought to alert ministers to destructive behaviors in multiple staff relationships.

How do you cope?

What handles can we offer you?

1. Build a trusting relationship.

2. Begin gentle, loving probing. "Charlie, I see this is your behavior and attitude...Are you willing to reflect on this and work at modifying it?"

3. Observe their response. Observe their willingness to work with you.

In integrating this chapter theologically, the authors call you to reflect on at least two sections of scripture.

1. The Bible speaks of "hardness of heart." One way of becoming hard hearted is by developing *personality rigidity*: when a person refuses to see a need to modify or change his life. Legalism frequently grows out of rigidity developed from unresolved stress. The Bible has much to say about the sources of stress.

2. In the story of Jesus with the rich young ruler, we see Jesus examining personal rigidity. "Show me you are *willing to change* by giving up your money" is the essence of Jesus' command. Many counselors, like Jesus, have had to watch an inflexible, hardened person walk away.

VII
Selecting and Growing a Church Staff

It is impossible to present an infallible list of what to look for in hiring a pastoral staff. However, you will find some useful suggestions on the following pages. In addition, behavior can change under the stress of the pastorate. Who doesn't dream of a litmus paper test to determine the perfect staff addition? Yet, even after companies have done a handwriting analysis, color chart, review of references, and psychiatric screening, the element of risk remains.

Before you see our lists of what we think is of general importance in hiring multiple staff--jot down your list of desirable qualities in staff persons:

_____

_____

_____

_____

_____

_____

_____

_____

_____

_____

_____

In *Leadership* magazine (Fall Quarter, 1982, pp. 99-104) Fred Smith lists six qualities he looks for in building a church staff:

He begins with character because of the vulnerability of the whole organization without it, and the difficulty of correcting weak character. Second, is intelligence. Then, flexibility. Fourth, is a person who is excited about learning. Team players and persons with a basic comfort in being reviewed, round out the list.

Our list looks something like this:

1. Determine the level of competence. This is difficult and tricky. Many people have been around great works, but you find out later they were in no way responsible for the work. They talk the talk, have insights, know the right people on a first name basis, but cannot do it themselves.

2. Faith. Do you perceive God in similar ways? Do you communicate in similar ways? Is their faith simplistic (an escape from the difficult) or integrated with the realities of life? Will people they serve get half truths that will not stand the test of crises?

3. Are they self starters, or do they have to be pushed and prodded? We have few management skills to prod a reluctant staff person.

4. Are they teachable? A disciple is a learner. As long as we are living, we are to go on learning. It is a frustrating experience to be linked with one who knows it all.

5. Mutual goals. If the church's and staff's goals are to serve the surrounding inner city, hiring someone with a primary focus on overseas missions will build conflict into the staff. Or, if the church's focus is evangelism, there should be careful thought before adding a person strongly oriented toward ecumenism.

6. One who knows how to problem solve. We

"He was traded to Valley Church for a music director and a youth pastor."

suggest you set up a few problems, and ask them for their style of resolving difficult situations in their special ministry, as well as inner staff relationships.

7. Always run a new pastor past the secretaries, and watch their ability to intuitively spot shallowness or phoniness. A community organization in the San Francisco bay area had a board of directors composed of thorough and competent leaders. They presented their selection for the new director to the secretaries. They had lunch and replied, "We can't trust this guy. He's hiding something." The directors were sure it was sour grapes, but delayed the public announcement for seven days and did a series of check outs. The police check revealed he had embezzled in his previous position.

8. Do not overlook the obvious. What is their style of private prayer? How and where are they sensitive to the social needs of people? What is their pattern of personal Bible study and worship?

9. Keeps confidences. God keeps confidences, and people speaking to a pastor expect confidences to be kept. It is a fact that people leave churches, reject the Christian faith, and reject God because of their disillusionment when a pastor passes along words spoken in private.

Different Grids to View Staff Growth

As a staff develops over weeks and years there are a number of visual images to reflect on.

One is to see the staff as a building with need for a careful foundation that will not collapse, plumbing that is functional, a boldness in design, built-in safety features, and an appearance that attracts people.

Another image is to see the church staff as butterflies emerging from the cocoon. See how incredibly fragile each one is, and how the ugly, hairy worm becomes a beautiful butterfly. The butterfly emerging from the cocoon must be given the freedom to struggle and not be rescued or its wings will never be strong enough to survive. In order to develop, the cocoon required the stability of the tree. What stability do we provide?

Still another image is to see the staff as an athletic team developing their communication skills with each other under pressure, constantly going over the fundamentals of Bible study, prayer, obedience; learning their positions; encouraging one another with words of affirmation; congratulating each other on jobs well done; studying the opposition; and sharing insights.

Essential Staffing Stages for a Church

The following organizations and staff stages of development are essential if a group is to survive and grow. No matter how "good" a purpose the church has, you must recognize the steps of growth in the church or you risk frustration and ineffectiveness.

Stage 1 is growth through drive. The beginning organization requires a vision, goal, or common purpose. It requires a rather highly energetic, autonomous, charismatic personality. Most small churches that become "big" began their growth under such a leader.

Most interdenominational camps had such a person at their inception. Interdenominational movements such as Young Life, World Vision, Campus Crusade, Bible Study Fellowship and others had a similar impetus. Even theological seminaries went through similar growth pains.

Danger comes as growth approaches Stage 2, and the charismatic type leader has difficulty adapting to new requirements for leadership.

The movement from Stage 1 to Stage 2 is often painful, frustrating, and slow.

Stage 2 is growth through organizational design. This level of growth requires administrative knowledge and training. The person in charge of this step or phase of growth must be more of a pragmatist than a dreamer. He must understand organization dynamics and be able to implement those structures that will best enable the growing organization to fulfill its goals.

At this level, the charismatic leader must be retrained, or a chief administrator or staff pastor must be added. What is essential is the nuts and bolts operation--rather than creating new goals.

Stage 3 is a growth-through-working-together design. This level requires skilled delegation. The span of control often becomes an issue at this point because one person can only supervise up to eight people. Leadership at this step requires a personality that can trust people, work through goals, exude warmth, empathy, and patience. These leaders must be able to focus on people, and not efficiency. An even temperament is crucial. At Stage 3, "I can no longer get my arms of control around the organization. It has become too big. I must give up some power and responsibility. My hands will never touch. Others must fill in the circle."

Stage 4 is growth through ongoing fulfillment of needs within the community. This level requires skilled coordination of many divisions and departments. The church may have a Christian school attached, senior citizens' apartment complex, around-the-clock counseling hot line center, radio or television ministry, printing and publishing division. How do we cut through red tape, work with computers, business design, and personnel policies? There is a need for able people to run these specialized services who will not tolerate an enthusiastic entrepreneur telling them what to do. Giving direction, yes; having all the answers, no.

VIII
Important Things a Senior Pastor Can Do For an Associate/Assistant

Introduction

We hope at this point that we have stressed the importance of healthy staff relations to the successful functioning of your church. Note Christ's impatience at the unwillingness of the disciples to work with conflict: at Gethsemene when they slept during his most needy moments; his return from the Mount of Transfiguration, and they are ineffective, lacking faith; his irritation at John wanting to call down fire and destroy a Samaritan village.

Paul used himself as a role model with his disciples, "Follow me, as I follow Christ," Jesus and Paul understood the importance of the process of working together, and they modeled concern, empathy, patience, and confrontation.

The senior pastor should be conscious of the role model he sets before others on the church staff and aiding them in understanding the reasons for the role.

1. One thing not learned in seminary is the "why" of decision making. Why do we worship the way we do? Why do we do funerals in a particular way? and weddings? Why do we do so little pastoral visitation or counseling? Why are we involved or not involved in community service clubs?

2. The senior pastor needs to communicate to staff where he is leading the church (like the captain of a ship telling the crew where the boat is headed and what detours to expect and why). A major obstacle often occurs at this point. Most pastors have a vision of where they want the church to go, but few of them have the administrative gifts necessary to lead the church in that direction. What is difficult for many pastors, staffs and boards to understand and accept is that the pastor does not have to do both--set the

course and steer the ship. He sets the course and tends to other things he does well.

3. It is helpful to recognize and learn to cope with inevitable past tapes in our lives.

If the senior pastor reminds a younger assistant of his stern father, the young assistant will probably build defenses right away.

Past tapes also go by the name of "transference," which is the psychological process where a person's expectations of, and emotional responses toward, a current relationship are just as they would respond to a relationship in the past. Transference is the phenomenon where ideas, emotions, attitudes, that you attached originally to one important person in your past--are now transferred to another person in your present. I prepare for my behavior with you based on a past relationship which sometimes is distorted and destructive. A past tape is when your assistant has been worked over by a senior pastor in his last church, and knows you will hurt him also. He operates on that bias, without being aware of it. He acts as if you are waiting for the perfect opportunity to "get him."

It's double trouble when the senior pastor (unaware of what he is doing) accepts the transference, and begins to relate to his assistants. For example, they may think of him as a father, so he treats them like children. They see him as tough and angry, so he takes on that role when he is with them.

4. It is important that the senior pastor not do what is done daily in the business world (and, all too frequently, in many churches) by using the secretary to destroy assistants. If the support staff cuts off communication, they will always reduce the assistant pastor to ineffectiveness until he leaves in despair.

5. Another helpful handle in understanding the staff relationship is to review similar dynamics in a marriage relationship. What are the techniques or patterns of communication? How does the staff support each other? (See page 54, *Communication: Key to Your*

"I bet the assistant pastor will be glad when his apprenticeship is over!"

Marriage, by H. Norman Wright, Regal Books, 1974, or *Caring Enough to Hear and be Heard*, by David Augsburger, Regal Books, 1982.

6. An ingredient for reflection is to discover how this person is emotionally nurtured. Do they need guarded time for reading, lots of affirmation, freedom to be creative, recognition?

It is important to communicate how you are important to me and to the church. Also, you need to communicate the joy of the staff teamwork, your trust in their judgment, and the staff's mutual ability to problem-solve.

7. Why not enjoy one another around a cup of coffee, or a meal, or non-work event? In the book, *Fire in Coventry*, Verney declares that renewal in the churches began when the clergy took time for enjoying each other in play.

8. Effective staff relationships are helped by mutually covering for each other. Any church staff person is extra vulnerable to a parish and community because the work is so visible and often under pressure circumstances--death, divorce, marriage, and various public meetings. Staff relationships are greatly strengthened when one staff member stops gossip, interprets the other in a positive light, and gives public affirmation.

Case Study: Conflict came in this particular congregation when the congregation began growing rapidly over a period of two years and the pastor felt that his gift was strictly preaching. He would have nothing to do with any other aspect of the church. The associate pastors had been accustomed to this senior pastor working with them in all aspects of the church. Conflict increased until the associates threatened to resign unless he became involved. He would not budge his position. After consultation--the church hired a well trained and previously successful business manager. He worked mostly with the associate pastors in other aspects of their work. This supported them enough to continue functioning.

IX
Important Things an Assistant Can Do For a Senior Pastor

Introduction

The success of any organization--be it the family, company, or church--is that every one must pull together. You may feel like the new kid on the block, or at the bottom of the pile, but think how one child can sabotage the whole family. One staff person can immobilize much of the church. The lack of cooperation from one division can paralyze a big company for months. Your spirit influences the whole team. One lineman misses his block, and the quarterback is flattened and a fumble can occur.

1. It helps for the assistant pastor to understand the senior pastor's personality type, and how to cope with it.

2. The assistant pastor needs to be supportive of the senior pastor's power structure, family, and goals.

Let us use the analogy of football again. At times the assistant or associate is the blocking back running interference for the pastor and his programs. At other times, he scouts for new talent. Then again, he reads the stands to see crowd reaction and the mood of the fans. He looks down from the tower with another perspective and sends in suggestions. Sometimes he deals with the press. At other times he carries the ball. On occasion, he replaces light bulbs in the stadium, and even shags loose balls. We are back to the servant concept in staff relationships!

3. Accountability of time is important. Sometimes pastors, as professionals, fall into the trap of thinking they can come into the office at 10:00 a.m. and leave at 2:00 pm. without giving account to anyone. We probably know of big name pastors who have modeled independence, and set precedence: three days a week in the office--the rest of the time in writing and

speaking and travel. There is cause for anger and misunderstanding when people give very little time accountability. Subtle sabotage from the staff is likely if you choose to hide your schedule from them. How often have you called a church to hear, "I don't know where the pastor is or what he is doing or when he'll be back. I'm sorry. Can I help you?" Mutual accountability is very helpful to good staff functioning.

4. There is an on-going need to communicate what is happening.

An intern worked in a church where the senior pastor wanted to know what events Junior High, High School, and College youth were going to be doing. Every Monday he took ten minutes to memorize the information, and during the week would pass along the specific details to any people he met in the community. Instead of saying--"Call the church"--he signed them up for youth camps right there and gave them a special invitation to a hay ride or skating party. The intern felt like he had a public relations director!

Consider sharing titles of books and magazines you are reading, content of studies you are leading, what things are keeping you from reaching your objectives, what you are feeling. Galatians 6:6, "Let him who is taught the word share all good things with him who teaches."

5. Recognize that the young intern or assistant is probably idealistic, a bit naive, and has an enormous need for affirmation. Seminary teaches idealism. You hear the best sermons of the best preachers, and no pastor you work with can measure up in the pulpit week after week.

6. It helps if an assistant pastor realizes that most senior pastors have very little isolation. This generation has developed endless vehicles for harassment--urban mass, automobiles, telephones, volumes of second-class mail. The senior pastor is the one we go to when we are angry at God. (After all, he is God's right hand man, isn't he?) No longer can he sit and make tents like Paul, spend a few days alone

in jail, take a couple of days to walk to the next city, or leisurely ride the boat to another village. The associate pastor can serve as a buffer and slow down potential burn out.

X
Resolving Pastor, Painful Staff Relationships

The "church personality" influences the relationship of the staff. As in the case of individual personalities, a group personality changes slowly and with much effort. What is the personality of your church?

- rigid, or flexible?
- warm and personable, or cold and formal and aloof?
- internal tension and division, or a spirit of cooperation?
- intellectualizing of feelings, or active interpersonal relations?
- stoical, or spontaneously joyful?
- unorganized, or over-organized?
- grandiose, or very humble?

Reflect on the history of this church. How has each pastor treated the congregation? How has the congregation treated each pastor, and why? How has the previous staff related to each other? What is the church's sense of community?

How did the apostle Paul resolve his painful past? He took a lot of time, perhaps three years in Arabia after his conversion near Damascus, and then additional time at Tarsus before being called to minister at Antioch. He constructively contrasted present and future life with his past. This is eloquently expressed in Philippians, chapter three.

Looking back...where and how can I find resolution from past painful staff experiences?

1. When you realize and accept as okay that at the time of that complicated, painful staff experience you did not have the necessary skills to cope well.

2. When you return in your mind to reevaluate the past experiences of pain, you not regress emotionally

to the age and skills you possessed then--but take who you are now back to those events.

3. Perhaps some confession and forgiveness is still needed on your part.

4. When you can see how God has used those past experiences to make you who you are today.

5. Differentiate between indignation and rage. The one who can approach problem solving at the point of indignation usually does better at resolution than the one who boils to the point of rage.

XI
Where is Hope?

Our theology of hope is that your personal staff experiences may not be "good" or "easy," yet God will use them (even the hurtful, destructive ones) for ultimate good.

Philippians 2:13, "For God is at work in you, both to will and to work for his good pleasure."

Romans 8:28, "We know that in everything God works for good for those who love him, who are called according to his purpose."

Genesis 50:20, "You meant it for evil, but God used it for good." Many years later, Joseph could see his painful past from a different perspective. His own brothers sought to destroy him, but God used that destructiveness to shape his life and the history of Israel.

Philippians 1:12, "I want you to know, brethren, that what has happened to me has really served to advance the gospel,"

We have numerous illustrations in the Bible where people had to spend lots of time and energy working through issues.

1. Jacob wrestled all night with an angel, but the result was a changed name and life.

2. In the book of Acts, Chapter 15, the issue of the Gentile circumcision was not resolved instantly by a vision or word from God. Verse 7 records, "And after there had been much debate..." That implies strenuous argument.

3. Also, in Acts 15, the missionary task force of the church doubled. Paul and Barnabas could not agree as to the wisdom of taking John Mark on another

missionary trip because of his abandoning them on the first trip.

Verse 39, "And there arose a sharp contention, so that they separated from each other;" As a result, Paul took Silas and Barnabas took John Mark--and *two* missionary teams went forth.

Where is hope? When one is able to see that successful staff relationships further the world-wide church. This is the theme of "purpose." Healthy staff relationships build the kingdom of God. This enables you and me to survive--to stick it out. Viktor E. Frankl says this "meaning concept" gives energy. This tremendous sense of importance and meaning is balanced by humility because when you leave, God will replace you and continue building his kingdom.

Where is hope? Hope comes when each staff member establishes a support system that listens, clarifies, affirms, communicates love, has mutual goals, and each knows where their individual contribution is and can identify it.

If you keep people isolated and lonely, then the unilateral, egocentric authorities can more easily implement their edicts uncontested. You set in motion a system for manipulation and exploitation. When pastors meet and share and problem solve, a new dynamic enters--bilateral authority.

Also, both senior and assistant pastor need different mentors apart from the church.

1. Moses could go to his father-in-law Jethro for help.

2. Joshua was under the tutelage of Moses for forty years.

3. Samuel had fellowship with the old priest Eli.

4. Hezekiah had the counsel of Isaiah.

5. The disciples were nurtured by Jesus for three

or more years.

Where is hope? Hope comes in grasping and practicing the biblical concept of *mutual submissiveness*. The *leader* is frequently an *enabler*. Good spiritual leadership in home or church involves a sensitivity to gifts God has given others and encouraging their use and development. The servant concept of leadership, which encourages others to reach their full potential in Christ needs to be revitalized.

Hebrews 12:1-2 does not say we are racing against each other. We each run the race God has set before us. Some run six miles, and some sixteen, and some run a greater distance. Some walk while others jog and a few sprint. Our goal is to run the cause that God has set before us, and not compare our assignment with another.

Hope comes from a church board or head of staff staffing to weaknesses, rather than to strengths. Kent R. Hunter in an article entitled, "A Model for Multiple Staff Management," describes staffing a church according to gifts. He had gifts of teaching and administration. Neil, the assistant, had gifts in counseling. Tony had gifts in education and counseling. Dave had the gift of celibacy, which gave him an independence and flexibility that none of the other staff had. Joann, called a deaconess, had the strongest gifts of mercy and helps. Frank was set free from administrative detail to exercise his gift of evangelism. So, with diversity of age, sex, race, and educational background, they were united in the attitude of servanthood, while exercising and developing their gifts. (p. 99, *Leadership Magazine*, Summer Quarter, 1981.)

Epilogue

What we have tried to do in this book:

First of all, we, the authors, have been involved in some very painful, difficult, distinctively different staff relationships. As we have spent money, time, energy, study, and prayer in resolving them, we experienced genuine hope for present and ongoing ministries.

Furthermore, we began to help a growing number of colleagues going through similar experiences. We desired something written to place in their hands. So we have put together our collective research and journeys. We hope this book is both helpful and hopeful.

The fall in Genesis 3 created the necessity to resolve problems. There are techniques for problem-solving in the same way there are techniques for Bible study. As the study of the scriptures requires effort, so the resolution of problems is an ongoing struggle. We urge you to give yourself permission to wrestle with conflict, so that irresolution will be dealt a lethal blow. With everything in us, we urge you to persevere in problem-solving staff relationships so that growth will occur. As Walter Trobish wrote, "It pays to suffer lover's grief." (*Love is a Feeling To Be Learned*, I.V. Press, p. 14.)

Bibliography

Augsburger, David, *Caring Enough to Confront*, Herald Press, Regal Books, 1973.

Augsburger, David, *Caring Enough to Forgive*, Regal Books, 1981.

Augsburger, David, *Caring Enough to Hear and Be Heard*, Regal Books, 1982.

Carter, Leslie, Meir, Paul, and Minirth, Frank, *Why Be Lonely?* Baker House, 1982.

Dayton, Ed and Engstrom, Ted, *The Anguish of Change*, World Vision, February 1982.

Dayton, Ed and Engstrom, Ted, *Power*, "Christian Leadership Letter," World Vision, October 1982.

Dobson, James, *Emotions, Can You Trust Them?*, Bantam Books (published by arrangement with Regal Books), 1982.

Hunt, Arthur, *Liking Life Under the Senior Pastor*, "Christianity Today," August 6, 1982.

Hunter, Kent, *A Model for Multiple Staff Management*, "Leadership," Summer Quarter 1981.

Lindquist, Stanley, *Reach Out...Become an Encourager*, Creation House, 1983.

Phillips-Jones, Linda, *Mentors and Proteges*, Arbor House, 1982.

Smith, David, *The Friendless American Male*, Regal Press, 1982.

Smith, Fred, *Building the Church Staff*, "Leadership," Fall Quarter 1982.

Verney, Stephen, *Fire in Coventry*, Revell, 1964.

Ron Wiebe received his M.S.W. degree at the University of Kansas, with post graduate work at the Menninger Foundation and Tulane University, including studies in family therapy, administration, and mental health consultation. He has served on the faculties of various universities for 16 years and has 20 years of experience in clinical practice, administration, organizational consultation (churches, missions, industry, community mental health facilities). He has been a member of the Boards of Directors for a number of national ministries.

About the Authors

Bruce Rowlison is a graduate of the University of Minnesota, with majors in Speech and English, and of Fuller Theological Seminary. He received his Doctor of Ministry degree from the Jesuit Theological Seminary in Berkeley, California. He is currently the pastor of the Gilroy Presbyterian Church in Gilroy, California.

He is the author of *Let's Talk About Your Wedding and Marriage* and *Creative Hospitality As A Means of Evangelism*.

BOOKS AVAILABLE FROM GREEN LEAF PRESS

—GOD IS LIGHT by Foster H. Shannon
ISBN 0-938462-000-8, 240 pages, Kivar cover $6.95
A fresh and unique approach to apologetics, thoroughly up-to-date. Persuasive presentation of the cause for Christianity.

—GOD'S GREEN LINIMENT by Lois Johnson Rew
ISBN 0-938462-02-4, 204 pages, Kivar cover $5.95
A gripping and delightful children's story of Alice, an Illinois farm girl of Swedish immigrant parents, her exciting adventures, dramatic recovery from polio, and warm family relationships.

—THUNDER OVER SCOTLAND: George Wishart, Mentor of John Knox by James William Baird
ISBN 0-938462-04-0, 206 pages, Kivar cover $7.95
An inspiring biographical novel of Scotland's earliest Protestant Reformer. George Wishart plowed the field that John Knox planted. Historical details are followed with meticulous accuracy.

—CREATIVE HOSPITALITY As A Means of Evangelism by Bruce A. Rowlison
ISBN 0-938462-03-2, 145 pages, Kivar cover $5.95
A challenging and convincing presentation of the gift of hospitality as an expression of Christian love and concern. Explores models, barriers, and helpful hints for hospitality.

—LET'S TALK ABOUT YOUR WEDDING AND MARRIAGE by Bruce Rowlison and George Hinn
ISBN 0-938462-01-6 $2.00
A 32-page attractive, practical new aid for wedding and marriage counseling for pastors and counselors.

—THE GREEN LEAF BIBLE SERIES, YEAR ONE: HEROES OF THE BIBLE, Genesis, Luke, Exodus, and Paul, Part I, Foster H. Shannon, Senior Editor
ISBN 0-938462-06-7, 174 pages, 8½x11, Kivar $12.50
A six-year Sunday School curriculum covering the entire Bible for first grade through adult. Arranged in quarterly segments with weekly outlines for Sunday School teachers.

—CHRISTIAN COMMITMENT by Edward John Carnell
ISBN 0-8010-2473-0 (Baker Book House) $9.95
    This classic of Protestant Evangelical scholarship presents a compelling case for the Christian gospel by means of convincing truths that all people are already committed to.

—CRUCIAL QUESTIONS IN APOLOGETICS
by Mark M. Hannah
ISBN 0-8010-4237-2 (Baker Book House) $5.95
    An illuminating discussion of the relationship between faith and reason in Christian belief. A brilliantly presented case for the continuity of general truth and biblical truth.

—THE GROWTH CRISIS IN THE AMERICAN CHURCH
by Foster H. Shannon
ISBN 0-87808-152-6 (William Carey Library) $4.95
    Presents both the rationale for sound church growth and the means for attaining growth within the ordinary Protestant church.

—THE WORD STUDY CONCORDANCE AND THE WORD STUDY NEW TESTAMENT by Ralph Winter, Ph.D.
ISBN-0-87808-751-6 (Tyndale/Wm. Carey Lib.) $34.95
    Why buy several concordances when one will do so well? An indispensable aid for students of the Greek New Testament keyed in such a way that Greek words and concepts are opened up even for those who have no first-hand knowledge of Greek.

Green Leaf Press, P.O. Box 6880, Alhambra, CA 91802

Please send me the books I have checked above. I enclose a check or money order. For orders under $7.00 please include 60¢ postage. Green Leaf Press pays shipping on orders over $7.00. Ship to:

Name_____

Address_____

City_____State_____Zip_____

Please charge my Mastercard ☐ or Visa ☐

Number_____Exp. date_____

Signature_____